everyday
mindfulness

everyday mindfulness

365 WAYS TO A CENTRED LIFE

Bounty
BOOKS

An Hachette UK Company
www.hachette.co.uk

First published in 2016 by Bounty Books,
a division of Octopus Publishing Group Ltd
Carmelite House
50 Victoria Embankment
London, EC4Y 0DZ

www.octopusbooks.co.uk

Copyright © Octopus Publishing Group Ltd 2016

ISBN: 978-0-75373-085-0

A CIP catalogue record for this book is available
from the British Library

Printed and bound in China

10 9 8 7 6 5 4 3 2

Design: Wide Open Studio
Publisher: Samantha Warrington
Design manager: Megan van Staden
Contributing editor: Emma Hill
Editor: Phoebe Morgan
Production controller: Sarah Kramer
Images: Shutterstock/Irtsya
Image, 26th August: Dreamstime/Realillusion

INTRODUCTION

Mindfulness (noun):
A mental state achieved by focusing one's awareness on the present moment, while calmly acknowledging and accepting one's feelings, thoughts, and bodily sensations.

Everyday Mindfulness provides a mindful exercise, idea or inspirational quote for every day of the year. Adopting a mindful lifestyle doesn't have to mean taking hours out of your day to meditate.

In fact, every situation you find yourself in presents an opportunity to practise mindfulness: waiting at the bus stop, queuing in a shop, even performing household chores…

Just taking a few minutes each day to ground yourself in the present moment can be hugely beneficial to both your physical and mental wellbeing.

Increasingly, research is suggesting that mindfulness can lower stress levels, blood pressure, improve your quality of sleep and so much more.

Developing the habit of daily mindfulness will likely improve your overall quality of life and your levels of happiness, as well as bringing a sense of inner peace.

Mindfulness can feel counterintuitive to our usual way. We are busy, so we rush. We have too much to do, so we multitask. Conversely, to be mindful is to slow down and focus on one task at a time.

You will actually improve your productivity if you can manage to do this and you will certainly live your life with a greater sense of calm.

To be mindful is to learn how to fully appreciate life's little pleasures and the most precious of moments that all too often pass by unnoticed when the mind is distracted.

Don't let another year slip through your fingers in the blink of an eye. Use this book as your guide, inspiration and motivation to embrace a year of mindful living.

THE BODY SCAN

The body scan meditation is a great place to start your mindfulness journey.

Make yourself comfortable, lying on your back on the floor or on your bed. Allow your eyes to close gently. Take a few moments to get in touch with the movement of your breath and the sensations in your body. When you are ready, begin by focusing your attention on the tips of your toes and then move up the body slowly, focusing on each body part as you go; the ball and heel of the foot. The sides and upper part of the foot. The ankle… As you breathe in, imagine the breath going down your body and into your toes. As you breathe out, imagine the breath going back up your body and out of your nose. Repeat this process of gentle awareness of each body part and sensation until you reach the top of your head.

"If you want
to conquer the
anxiety of life, live
in the moment, live
in the breath."

– AMIT RAY

"Mindfulness is simply being aware of what is happening right now without wishing it were different; enjoying the pleasant without holding on when it changes (which it will); being with the unpleasant without fearing it will always be this way (which it won't)."

– JAMES BARAZ

MINDFUL COMMUNICATION

Today, practise bringing your mindful attention to your interactions with others. Focus on making eye contact with the people you communicate with, on really seeing them.

"Respond; don't react. Listen; don't talk. Think; don't assume."

– RAJI LUKKOOR

WAKE UP GENTLY

Try keeping your eyes closed for a few minutes after you wake. Focus on your breathing and on the sensations around you – the softness of your duvet, the smell of the sheets, distant sounds from outside the window…

TRANSFORMATIONAL LAUNDRY

Transform chores into mindful tasks by slowing them down and really paying attention. When doing the laundry, notice the feel and textures of the fabrics and how fresh they smell. Pay attention to the patterns and colours and the way they are affected by the light of the room. Make folding into a sort of yoga practice and move with mindfulness, attentive to each fold. This keeps you in tune with the moment, with yourself and your space – all functioning in harmony.

"If you are mentally somewhere else, you miss real life."

– BYRON KATIE

"My goal today is to live in a state of grace and lightness. I will not invite struggle or drama. I will say yes more and smile often."

– KIMBERLEY BLAINE

CREATE A "TO-BE" LIST

This is an alternative to a to-do list. Halfway through the day, pause and take a minute to ask, "How am I being right now?" Curt, or understanding? Defensive, or open-minded? Dismissive, or kind? Turn your "to-be" list into a goal and try to maintain it on a discreet post-it on your desk, or wherever you are likely to see it, to keep your intentions in check.

"The present moment is filled with joy and happiness. If you are attentive, you will see it."

– THÍCH NHẤT HẠNH

DO NOTHING

Even if it's just for five minutes, sit for that five minutes and do… nothing. Sit silently in a comfortable chair or in a sunny spot outside, if possible without mobile phones or other distractions near you. Become still. Bring your full awareness into the present moment. All that exists for you is the here and now. You may be amazed at how pleasurable and satisfying it is just to "be", and how much taking just five minutes from your day will give back to your life as a whole.

"Allow yourself to rest. Your soul speaks to you in the quiet moments in between your thoughts."

– ANONYMOUS

MINDFUL WALKING

Walking can give you a chance to spend time being mindful without taking any extra time out of your day. Wherever you are walking to or from today, turn it into a meditative exercise. Walk slowly, paying attention to the sensations on the soles of your feet. Notice as each part of the sole, from heel to toe, touches the ground. Lifting, moving, placing. Lifting, moving, placing. Notice how the body moves as you walk. Walk with awareness. One step at a time. Notice any thoughts that arise and let them be.

"Walk as if you are kissing the Earth with your feet."

– THÍCH NHẤT HẠNH

"Carpe Diem.
Seize the day."

- HORACE

"If you don't love yourself, you cannot love others. If you have no compassion for yourself, you cannot develop compassion for others."

– DALAI LAMA

TAKE 5

Every now and then throughout the day, challenge yourself to find five things that are part of your present experience.

First notice five things that you can see with your eyes. They don't necessarily have to be interesting; it might just be a table, the carpet or a cup in front of you. The aim is simply to bring your full awareness to your experience now in the present moment.

Then notice five things you can hear. Keep listening until you've distinguished five different sounds.

Then notice five things you can feel with your body. These might be the material of your clothes, a slight breeze or even tension in your neck.

"Don't keep allowing the same things to upset you. Life's too short to live that way."

– JOEL OSTEEN

"To see a world in a grain of sand
and heaven in a wild flower,
Hold infinity in the palm of your
hand and eternity in an hour."

– WILLIAM BLAKE

"Mindfulness is the aware, balanced acceptance of the present experience. It isn't more complicated than that. It is being open to or receiving the present moment, pleasant or unpleasant, just as it is, without either clinging to it or rejecting it."

– SYLVIA BOORSTEIN

"Life isn't as serious as the mind makes it out to be."

– ECKHART TOLLE

"The best way to capture moments is to pay attention. This is how we cultivate mindfulness. Mindfulness means being awake. It means knowing what you are doing."

– JON KABAT-ZINN

BE HERE NOW

This great piece of advice comes from the well-known spiritual teacher, Ram Dass.

We should ask ourselves: Where am I?

Answer: Here.

Then ask ourselves: What time is it?

Answer: Now.

Keep repeating until you really feel grounded in the present moment.

"Life can be found only in the present moment. The past is gone, the future is not yet here, and if we do not go back to ourselves in the present moment, we cannot be in touch with life."

— THÍCH NHẤT HẠNH

GET UP EARLY TO WATCH THE SUNRISE

The thought of getting up at the crack of dawn may be far from relaxing for many of us, but if you make the effort to do this you will feel revived and refreshed throughout the day as well as carrying a stronger sense of awareness and inner peace. Contemplate the sunrise, absorb the beauty of its colours, notice every aspect of the changing light, embrace the start of a new day. Whatever tasks lie in the day ahead, for these moments let your thoughts be still.

"Thoughts are slow and deep and golden in the morning."

– JOHN STEINBECK

"Forget about the past. It does not exist, except in your memory. Drop it. And stop worrying about how you're going to get through tomorrow. Life is going on right here, right now – pay attention to that and all will be well."

– NEALE DONALD WALSCH

"The moment one gives close attention to anything, even a blade of grass, it becomes a mysterious, awesome, indescribably magnificent world in itself."

– HENRY MILLER

THE MINDFUL TEA MEDITATION

Wrap both your hands around your mug of tea (or other warm beverage). Focus on the warmth radiating through the mug into your hands and breathe deeply. Notice how comforting it is to hold this warm mug between your hands – soothing and relaxing. Really pay attention and breathe deeply for a couple of minutes. Then take your first sip and savour the taste. Focus your mind on the taste. Be aware of how much you enjoy this drink. How the liquid flows over your tongue and down your throat, leaving this wonderful taste that you so appreciate in your mouth.

"Drink your tea slowly and reverently, as if it is the axis on which the world earth revolves – slowly, evenly, without rushing towards the future; live the actual moment. Only this moment is life."

– THÍCH NHẤT HẠNH

CHANGE
YOUR ROUTINE

Drive a different way to work, reverse the order in which you get ready in the morning or eat something new for breakfast. It's amazing how revitalizing this simple exercise can be.

"Inner peace is the key: if you have inner peace, the external problems do not affect your deep sense of peace and tranquility. Without this inner peace, no matter how comfortable your life is materially, you may still be worried, disturbed, or unhappy because of circumstances."

– DALAI LAMA

LABEL YOUR WORRIES

When you find yourself worrying about something today, consciously stop and label what you are doing as "just worrying." Then bring your attention back to your breath or simply change the subject of your thinking. Every time you catch yourself worrying, just label it again and change the subject.

"We spend precious hours fearing the inevitable. It would be wise to use that time adoring our families, cherishing our friends and living our lives."

– MAYA ANGELOU

"If you surrender completely to the moments as they pass, you live more richly those moments."

– ANNE MORROW LINDBERGH

"Sometimes you need to take a break from everyone and spend time alone, to experience, appreciate and love yourself."

– ROBERT TEW

"Right where you are is where you need to be. Don't fight it! Don't run away from it! Stand firm! Take a deep breath. And another. And another. Now, ask yourself: Why is this in my world? What do I need to see?"

– IYANLA VANZANT

TECH TIMEOUT

Technology brings lots of incredible benefits to our lives, but sometimes we need to switch off in order to quieten our thoughts. Today, empower yourself by taking a break from technology for one hour. Mobile phones included.

"Learn to get in touch with the silence within yourself and know that everything in this life has a purpose."

– ELISABETH KÜBLER-ROSS

A SPACE FOR YOU

Today, create a space in your house that is just for you. A calm
haven from both the outside world and the comings and goings
of the rest of your household. Choose a few of your favourite
items – maybe paintings or photographs that make you feel
calm or happy – to decorate the space. Maybe a comfortable
chair or cushion to sit on, a scented candle, your favourite book.
Whatever makes it feel calm, inviting and just for you.

"I don't have to chase extraordinary moments to find happiness. It's right in front of me if I'm paying attention and practising gratitude."

– BRENÉ BROWN

HARNESS THE HAND-MIND CONNECTION

One of the physical symptoms of stress is that it pulls the blood out of your toes and fingers and sends it to your internal organs. As a calming practice, immerse your hands in warm water to open up the blood vessels and trick your brain out of its stressful state.

"You must live in the present, launch yourself on every wave, find your eternity in each moment. Fools stand on their island opportunities and look toward another land. There is no other land, there is no other life but this."

— HENRY DAVID THOREAU

"Do every act of
your life as though
it were the very last
act of your life."

— MARCUS AURELIUS

"I change my life when I change my thinking. I am Light. I am Spirit. I am a wonderful, capable being. And it is time for me to acknowledge that I create my own reality with my thoughts. If I want to change my reality, then it is time for me to change my mind."

– LOUISE HAY

"There are always flowers for those who want to see them."

– HENRI MATISSE

OBSERVE YOUR THOUGHTS

To start, focus your attention on your breathing. Simply pay attention to what it feels like in your body as you breathe slowly in and then slowly breathe out. Now shift your attention to your thoughts. Try to view them as simply thoughts – they are only objects in your mind. They are just events happening inside your mind. Notice them enter your consciousness, develop, and then float away. You don't have to hold onto or follow your thoughts. Just let them arise and disappear on their own.

"If you empty yourself of yesterday's sorrows, you will have much more room for today's joy."

– JENNI YOUNG

MAKE THE EVERYDAY MAGICAL

Find a bit of magic in your day. It may be the sound of the rain, the laughter of a loved one, the clouds in the sky or a quiet moment alone. Whatever it is – and however small – make the magic moment count. Acknowledge it, appreciate it, embrace it.

"Why do they not teach you that time is a finger snap and an eye blink, and that you should not allow a moment to pass you by without taking joyous, ecstatic note of it, not wasting a single moment of its swift, breakneck circuit?"

– PAT CONROY

"What day is it?"

"It's today," squeaked Piglet.

"My favourite day," said Pooh."

– A.A.MILNE

AN EXERCISE IN COLOUR

Choose a colour and decide to notice that colour as you go about your day. Every time you notice the colour, stop and acknowledge it. This will slow your thoughts and place you in the present moment.

"The secret of health for both mind and body is not to mourn for the past, worry about the future, or anticipate troubles, but to live in the present moment wisely and earnestly."

– BUDDHA

"When you have an intense contact of love with nature or another human being, like a spark, then you understand that there is no time and that everything is eternal."

– PAULO COELHO

DRIVE MINDFULLY

Driving becomes a habit; however, there is a lot that goes into it. Next time you go for a drive, be mindful of the sights around you. Turn off the radio. Become aware of the noise your car makes as you accelerate or decelerate, the way the air conditioner or heater feels against your skin, or any other sensation associated with driving. You will bring a renewed sense of calm to any car journey.

"Live with intention.
Walk to the edge.
Listen hard.
Practise wellness.
Play with abandon.
Laugh.
Choose with no regret.
Appreciate your friends.
Continue to learn.
Do what you love.
Live as if this is all there is."

– MARY ANNE RADMACHER

"Stop acting as if life is a rehearsal.
Live this day as if it were your last.
The past is over and gone.
The future is not guaranteed."

– WAYNE DYER

"The only true thing is what's in front of you right now."

– RAMONA AUSUBEL

BRUSH YOUR TEETH MINDFULLY

Today when you brush your teeth, pay attention to what you are doing. Feel your feet grounded on the bathroom floor. Notice the feeling of the bristles of the toothbrush on your gums, the sound of the brush against your teeth, the taste of the toothpaste and the movement of your arm as you brush. Use all of your senses and as your mind wanders, bring it back to the sensations of brushing your teeth.

"Begin doing what you want to do now. We are not living in eternity. We have only this moment, sparkling like a star in our hand and melting like a snowflake."

– FRANCIS BACON SR.

"Looking at beauty in the world is the first step of purifying the mind."

– DR. AMIT RAY

"Compassion is not complete if it does not include oneself."

– ALLAN LOKOS

"There are only two ways to live your life. One is as though nothing is a miracle. The other is as though everything is a miracle."

– ALBERT EINSTEIN

"The past is the past and has nothing to do with you.
It has nothing to do with right now.
Do not let anything from your past inhibit you in this present moment.
Start over. Start fresh. Each day.
Each hour, if it serves you.
Heck, each minute. Just get going."

– NEALE DONALD WALSCH

DECLUTTER

Set some time aside today to declutter an area of your home or workspace. Although it may seem overwhelming at first, doing this can actually be as peaceful as a meditation. Clutter is a way of holding onto the past, or fearing the future. Letting go of clutter is a way to live more mindfully and in the present.

"Clutter stops the flow of positive energy in your space and ultimately in your life."

– JAYME BARRETT

COMMUTE MINDFULLY

Instead of wishing the journey away, embrace the time that it has afforded you to sit and be. Be mindful of your emotions as they rise and fall, come and go. Recognise the frustration, anger, impatience that may arise, but rather than thinking about them, judging them, or analysing them, simply acknowledge them.

"Rivers know this:
there is no hurry.
We shall get there
some day."

– A.A. MILNE

"I deserve the best and I accept the best now."

– LOUISE HAY

INDIAN HEAD MASSAGE

Take 10 minutes today to give yourself a simple three-step Ayurvedic Indian head massage. First rub your temples with your fingertips in a gentle, circular pattern. For the second step, "shampoo" the scalp. Massage the entire scalp in small circles with gentle fingertips. Begin at the temples and move towards the back of the head. Finish by combing the scalp; place your fingertips at the hairline, and comb over the top of the head down towards the neck and shoulders.

"Breathe. Let go. And remind yourself that this very moment is the only one you know you have for sure."

– OPRAH WINFREY

"Listening is the way. Listening is the beginning of all progress."

– BRYANT MCGILL

BE MINDFUL WITH MONEY

Living in the present means focusing on one financial decision at a time, as and when it arises. This will allow you to make a better decision about money, no matter how important. You can decide at that moment if it makes more sense to save or spend. So today, before you buy anything ask yourself: "Do I really need this? Should I spend this money right now or wait?"

"When you look at the sun during your walking meditation, the mindfulness of the body helps you to see that the sun is in you; without the sun there is no life at all and suddenly you get in touch with the sun in a different way."

– THÍCH NHẤT HẠNH

"It's not what you look at that matters, it's what you see."

– HENRY DAVID THOREAU

"What you think,
you become.
What you feel,
you attract.
What you imagine,
you create."

– UNKNOWN

"What is life? It is the flash of a firefly in the night. It is the breath of a buffalo in the wintertime. It is the little shadow which runs across the grass and loses itself in the sunset."

– BLACKFOOT

"You've got this life and while you've got it, you'd better kiss like you only have one moment, try to hold someone's hand like you will never get another chance to, look into people's eyes like they're the last you'll ever see, watch someone sleeping like there's no time left, jump if you feel like jumping, run if you feel like running, play music in your head when there is none, and eat cake like it's the only one left in the world!"

- C. JOYBELL C.

"Like a child standing in a beautiful park with his eyes shut tight, there's no need to imagine trees, flowers, deer, birds, and sky; we merely need to open our eyes and realize what is already here, who we already are."

– BO LOZOFF

LAUGH

Laughing brings us into the present moment
in a mindful way and is a great stress reliever.

"The most wasted of all days is one without laughter."

— NICOLAS CHAMFORT

DANCE

Try a dance class – nothing brings your mind faster into the present moment than when you're trying to get your body to move to a rhythm.

STOLEN MOMENTS

The concept of wasted time does not exist for a mindful person. Every spare moment can be used for meditation. Feeling irritated while queuing at the post office, meditate on irritation. Sitting anxiously in the doctor's waiting room, meditate on your anxiety. Bored waiting at the bus stop, meditate on boredom. Try to stay alert and aware throughout the day. Be mindful of exactly what is taking place right now. Today, use every spare second to be mindful. Use all the moments you can.

"Your mind is your instrument. Learn to be its master and not its slave."

– REMEZ SASSON

MONOTASK

Do one thing at a time. There is a growing body of evidence that suggests multitasking makes us less efficient, less effective, more stressed and more likely to make mistakes. Maintaining focus and interest on one task at a time is not easy, but start practising today.

"Today… spend more time with people who bring out the best in you, not the stress in you."

– UNKNOWN

"Smile, breathe
and go slowly."

- THÍCH NHẤT HẠNH

"One day you will wake up and realize that life has passed you by, that your dreams of today are gone, that the things you wanted are no longer there. Not today. Not now. Not your life. This is the day where you take control and create your future. Life isn't about waiting, hoping or wishing. It is about creating, doing and truly living. Today is that day."

– BRAD GAST

"There are far too many people who waste their time telling themselves that they don't have enough time."

– UNKNOWN

DON'T ANSWER YOUR PHONE IMMEDIATELY

Let it ring a couple of times as you collect
your thoughts and prepare to answer.
Think about the person calling.
What do they look like?
What frame of mind are they in?

HUGGING MEDITATION

You can practise this Buddhist hugging meditation with a loved one, or even with a tree. First bow to recognise the presence of each other and enjoy three deep, conscious breaths to bring yourself fully there. Open your arms and begin hugging, holding each other for three in-and-out breaths. With the first breath, be aware that you are present in this very moment and that you are happy. With the second breath, be aware that the other is present in this moment and that he or she is happy as well. With the third breath, be aware that you are here together, right now on this earth, and feel deep gratitude and happiness for that togetherness. Then release the other person and bow to each other to show thanks.

"Peace begins
when expectation
ends."

– SRI CHINMOY

TAKE A BATH

Today, take time out to wallow in a hot bath. Make your bathroom a haven of peace and calm. Banish your smart phone and light candles; use your favourite bubble bath or oil. Lie back and feel the warm water envelop your body. Focus on the sensations of warmth, inhale the scent of your bath products and observe how the candlelight reflects in the bubbles.

"In today's rush, we all think too much, seek too much, want too much and forget the joy of just being."

– ECKHART TOLLE

"Fear keeps us focused on the past or worried about the future. If we can acknowledge our fear, we can realize that right now we are okay. Right now, today, we are still alive, and our bodies are working marvellously. Our eyes can still see the beautiful sky. Our ears can still hear the voices of our loved ones."

– THÍCH NHẤT HẠNH

"Don't seek, don't search, don't ask, don't knock, don't demand – relax."

– OSHO

"We're all just walking each other home."

– RAM DASS

PEBBLE IN YOUR POCKET

Such a simple thing, and yet something that Zen masters the world over do, is to keep a pebble in a pocket. Do this and each time you put your hand in your pocket, hold the pebble gently and let it serve as a reminder to pause, smile and calmly breathe in and out.

"Write it on your heart that every day is the best day in the year."

– RALPH WALDO EMERSON

"The mind is everything. What we think, we become."

– BUDDHA

"Mindfulness is about being fully awake in our lives. It is about perceiving the exquisite vividness of each moment. We also gain immediate access to our own powerful inner resources for insight, transformation, and healing."

– JON KABAT-ZINN

EXERCISE MINDFULLY

Exercising mindfully is an incredibly powerful stress reliever. When you're working out, be fully in the present moment. This is your time to focus completely on yourself. Bring awareness to your breath and the physical capabilities of your body. Feel every stretch deeply and commit to giving every move your all. When you focus on what you're doing, you improve the quality of your movement and, as a result, the quality of your overall workout. Feel your own strength and power as you exercise.

"Your vision will become clear
only when you look into your heart.
Who looks outside, dreams. Who
looks inside, awakens."

– CARL JUNG

"Don't underestimate the value of doing nothing, of just going along, listening to all the things you can't hear, and not bothering."

— A.A. MILNE

LISTEN TO MUSIC

Really listen. Bring your attention to the sensations of sound and feeling as the piece begins. If your attention wanders, just gently remind yourself to return to the sounds and sensations of the music. If you can focus your mind entirely on that song and where it takes you, then you can transform your listening experience into a meditative experience.

"How we spend our days is of course how we spend our lives."

– ANNIE DILLARD

"Finish every day and be done with it.
You have done what you could.
Some blunders and absurdities,
no doubt, crept in.
Forget them as soon as you can,
tomorrow is a new day;
begin it well and serenely,
with too high a spirit to be cumbered
with your old nonsense."

– RALPH WALDO EMERSON

TRAFFIC LIGHT EXERCISE

Each time you have to stop at a red traffic light today, instead of being frustrated, use this still time to engage in a mindful practice. Bring focus to your breathing and give thanks for the car you are in/for the job you are driving to/for the friend you are on your way to visit…

"Leave your front door and back door open. Let your thoughts come and go. Just don't serve them tea."

– SHUNRYŪ SUZUKI

CLEANING

When cleaning your home, notice any feelings of resistance
and urges to get it done as quickly as possible. Then focus on
the doing, not the getting done. The motion of simple tasks can
make you more attentive and calm – the back and forth of the
vacuum cleaner, for example. Chores can be meditative, just
so long as you're not thinking about how much you hate them.
There is much comfort and peace to be found in repetitive tasks.

"If you clean the floor with love, you have given the world an invisible painting."

– OSHO

"Forever is composed of nows."

– EMILY DICKINSON

"We have only now, only this single eternal moment opening and unfolding before us, day and night."

– JACK KORNFIELD

PICK A PROMPT TO REMIND YOU TO BE MINDFUL

Choose a cue that you encounter on a regular basis to shift your brain into mindful mode. For instance, you might pick a certain door you walk through or a picture on the wall, or use drinking tea or coffee as a reminder.

"Remember this…
that very little is
needed to make a
happy life."

– MARCUS AURELIUS

LEAVES IN THE STREAM MEDITATION

Whilst sitting quietly, bring your focus to your breath. Start to notice the thoughts that come into your mind. As you notice each thought, imagine putting those words onto a leaf as it floats by on a stream. Place each thought that you notice onto a leaf, and watch it drift on by. There's no need to look for the thoughts, or to remain alert waiting for them to come. Just let them come, and when they do, place them onto a leaf.

"There will never be a time when your life is not this moment."

– DEEPAK CHOPRA

"All of human unhappiness comes from one single thing: not knowing how to remain at rest in a room."

– BLAISE PASCAL

"Just as trees shed their leaves
in winter and renew themselves,
the mind can shed its prejudices,
barriers and renew itself."

– RADHA BURNIER

"Mindfulness helps you go home to the present. And every time you go there and recognise a condition of happiness that you have, happiness comes."

– THÍCH NHẤT HẠNH

"Each morning
we are born
again. What we
do today is what
matters most."

– BUDDHA

"You can't stop the waves, but you can learn to surf."

– JON KABAT-ZINN

"Your calm mind
is the ultimate
weapon against
your challenges.
So relax."

– BRYANT MCGILL

"Meditation practice isn't about trying to throw ourselves away and become something better, it's about befriending who we are."

- PEMA CHÖDRÖN

"Concentrate all your thoughts on the task at hand. The sun's rays do not burn until brought into focus."

– ALEXANDER GRAHAM BELL

"Sometimes, if you stand on the bottom rail of a bridge and lean over to watch the river slipping slowly away beneath you, you will suddenly know everything there is to be known."

−A.A. MILNE

"When I heard the sound of the bell ringing, there was no bell, and there was no I—there was only the ringing."

– UNKNOWN

ASK FOR WHAT YOU WANT

It's often difficult to confront certain situations in any relationship, whether with a partner, a sibling or your boss. Today, bring to mind something you have been meaning to approach but have not had the courage to. Take several calming deep breaths. Feel your inner strength expand on the in-breath and your fear be dispelled on the out-breath. Feel yourself growing taller and more courageous with each in-breath. Now go and ask for what you want.

"People usually consider walking on water or in thin air a miracle. But I think the real miracle is not to walk either on water or in thin air, but to walk on earth. Every day we are engaged in a miracle which we don't even recognise: a blue sky, white clouds, green leaves, the black, curious eyes of a child – our own two eyes. All is a miracle."

—THÍCH NHẤT HẠNH

LET GO OF RESENTMENT

If you have an ill feeling towards another, today is the day to let it go. Sit in a comfortable position and bring awareness to your breathing. Focus on inhaling warm, open thoughts and dispelling negative ones. Bring to mind the person you feel resentment towards and direct loving thoughts towards them. Say out loud, "I wish love, health, peace and happiness for (insert name)." Although this may feel awkward at first, the feelings of peace and love will eventually replace any negative ones.

"Do not let the behaviour of others destroy your inner peace."

– DALAI LAMA

"Many people are alive but don't touch the miracle of being alive."

– THÍCH NHẤT HẠNH

"The practice of mindfulness begins in the small, remote cave of your unconscious mind and blossoms with the sunlight of your conscious life, reaching far beyond the people and places you can see."

– EARON DAVIS

"Always hold fast to the present.
Every situation, indeed every
moment, is of infinite value,
for it is the representative of a
whole eternity."

– JOHANN WOLFGANG VON GOETHE

A SIMPLE 5-MINUTE MEDITATION

Set a timer for 5 minutes. Lay on a flat, comfortable surface. Put one hand on your stomach, and one hand on your chest. Close your eyes. Slowly inhale deeply, focusing on breathing so deeply that you feel your stomach rise. Continue to inhale until you feel that your lungs are like balloons full of air, ready to pop. Count to 10 as you inhale. Slowly exhale, allowing all breath to exit your lungs and feeling your stomach as it returns to resting state. Strive to reach a total of 10 counts per exhale. Focus on this inhalation and exhalation pattern for the next 5 minutes.

"Be happy in the moment, that's enough. Each moment is all we need, no more."

– MOTHER TERESA

"In this moment,
there is plenty of time.
In this moment,
you are precisely as you should be.
In this moment,
there is infinite possibility."

– VICTORIA MORAN

SHIATSU
SELF MASSAGE

Use this Japanese massage technique, where the energy
channels (meridians) are stimulated by finger pressure.
For relaxation, hold your foot with thumbs pressing into
the sole and rub vigorously across the sole.

"Carry me away
on a song in the breeze,
to the place where love
grows on trees.
Let me fly like a dove
to a land way above,
so I can float with the whispers
above the surf on the seas."

– CHARLOTTE HILL

"Peace is the result of retraining your mind to process life as it is, rather than as you think it should be."

–WAYNE DYER

"When I dance, I dance; when I sleep, I sleep; yes, and when I walk alone in a beautiful orchard, if my thoughts drift to far-off matters for some part of the time for some other part I lead them back again to the walk, the orchard, to the sweetness of this solitude, to myself."

– MICHEL DE MONTAIGNE

GET BACK TO NATURE

Today, plant a seed or a bulb. If you have a garden, take time out to prepare your soil, dig in the earth and literally feel yourself grounded. Equally, you could plant a seed in a pot to place on a windowsill. Water the seed and watch it grow over time. Rejoice in nurturing nature in this small yet precious way.

"Start living right here, in each present moment. When we stop dwelling on the past or worrying about the future, we're open to rich sources of information we've been missing out on–information that can keep us out of the downward spiral and poised for a richer life."

– MARK WILLIAMS

EAT LUNCH OUTSIDE

Make the effort to eat lunch outside today. Savour each mouthful in your mindful eating, relish every flavour whilst enjoying the air in your lungs and the breeze against your skin. If you're unable to get out then at least try to sit near an open window.

"There's only one reason why you're not experiencing bliss at this present moment, and it's because you're thinking or focusing on what you don't have…. But, right now, you have everything you need to be in bliss."

– ANTHONY DE MELLO

TAKE A
POWER SNOOZE

At some point today take 10 minutes out for a reviving catnap. Make yourself comfortable and bring awareness to your breathing. Notice any noise around you and let the sounds sink into the distant background. Feel yourself removed from them. Allow your body to become heavy, sinking into the chair or bed. Let your thoughts drift and your body relax entirely. If you manage to drop off, you will feel refreshed and revived on waking. It is advisable to set a timer before you begin!

"If you are depressed, you are living in the past. If you are anxious, you are living in the future. If you are at peace, you are living in the present."

– LAO TZU

"Between stimulus and response there is a space. In that space is our power to choose our response. In our response lies our growth and our freedom."

– VIKTOR FRANKL

MEDITATE ON A RAINDROP

Or if it isn't raining, on a water droplet in the shower or bath. Wherever it may be – running down the window of a bus, say – take a moment to contemplate its perfection, its movement down the window or shower screen. Notice how it reflects the light, the speed at which it travels, its shifting shape. Contemplate where its journey began and where it will end.

"The range of what we think and do is limited by what we fail to notice. And because we fail to notice that we fail to notice, there is nothing we can do to change until we notice how failing to notice shapes our thoughts and deeds."

– R.D. LAING

"You need to learn how to select your thoughts just the same way you select your clothes every day. This is a power you can cultivate."

– ELIZABETH GILBERT

"I opened two gifts
this morning. They
were my eyes."

– UNKNOWN

"Meditation can help us embrace
our worries, our fear, our anger;
and that is very healing.
We let our own natural capacity
of healing do the work."

– THÍCH NHẤT HẠNH

"The creation of a thousand forests is in one acorn."

– RALPH WALDO EMERSON

WRITE A STREAM OF CONSCIOUSNESS JOURNAL

This is something you could do either in the morning to clear your head in preparation for the day, or at bedtime to empty your mind of clutter before sleep. Set a timer for five minutes and in this time write down all of your tumbling thoughts. Whatever comes into your mind, write it down. Just relax your mind, let the thoughts come and your pen flow easily across the page.

"Rule your mind
or it will rule you."

– BUDDHA

"Nothing can bring you peace but yourself."

– RALPH WALDO EMERSON

"I can't change the direction of the wind, but I can adjust my sails to always reach my destination."

– JIMMY DEAN

"Feelings are just visitors, let them come and go."

– MOOJI

"Mindfulness helps us freeze the frame so that we can become aware of our sensations and experiences as they are, without the distorting coloration of socially conditioned responses or habitual reactions."

– BHANTE HENEPOLA GUNARATANA

STRETCH YOUR BODY

At intervals throughout today, stop whatever you are doing to stretch your body. Choose whichever stretching moves you prefer and are appropriate for where you are. Simply stretching each arm across your body using the pull of your opposite hand, or rolling your head in a circle to stretch your neck, will be effective in bringing awareness back to your body.

THE 50/10 RULE

Today, for every 50 minutes you spend on a task,
take 10 minutes out to refocus your mind.

"When you love someone, the best thing you can offer is your presence. How can you love if you are not there?"

– THÍCH NHẤT HẠNH

"Everything we do is infused with the energy with which we do it. If we're frantic, life will be frantic. If we're peaceful, life will be peaceful."

– MARIANNE WILLIAMSON

"Mindful self-compassion can be learned by anyone. It's the practice of repeatedly evoking good will toward ourselves, especially when we're suffering – cultivating the same desire that all living beings have to live happily and free from suffering."

– CHRISTOPHER GERMER

"Worrying doesn't take away tomorrow's troubles, it takes away today's peace."

–ANONYMOUS

"It is never too late to be what you might have been."

– GEORGE ELIOT

"Pause and remember — the peace you seek begins with you! When you consciously and consistently choose peace in your words and actions, more peace will appear in your life. Stop blaming everything and everyone outside of you. Make peace within your priority."

– JENNI YOUNG

TODAY'S TO-DO LIST

inhale

exhale

inhale

exhale

inhale

exhale

inhale

exhale

A MINDFUL PROMPT

The hardest thing about mindfulness can be remembering to do it. Choose a prop to take to work, or wherever you will see it frequently throughout the day, maybe a favourite photograph or a plant. Use the prop as a prompt to be mindful and bring yourself into the present moment.

TRACK YOUR DAILY ACCOMPLISHMENTS

As the day concludes, find yourself a quiet space and write a list of everything you have achieved today. Remember to think moments, not miracles.

"As we encounter new experiences with a mindful and wise attention, we discover that one of three things will happen to our new experience: it will go away, it will stay the same, or it will get more intense. Whatever happens does not really matter."

– JACK KORNFIELD

"I believe in
living today.
Not in yesterday,
nor in tomorrow."

– LORETTA YOUNG

"Change your
thoughts and
you change
your world."

– NORMAN VINCENT PEALE

"What lies behind you and what lies in front of you pales in comparison to what lies inside of you."

– RALPH WALDO EMERSON

MOOD SURF

Throughout the day, check into your mood. Bring awareness
to your breathing, then tap into how you are feeling. Angry?
Tired? Frustrated? Bored? Whatever your mood, simply notice it,
acknowledge it and then return to your task. This is a simple and
effective way to break the cycle of unchecked negative moods.

"Stop waiting for Friday, for summer, for someone to fall in love with you, for life. Happiness is achieved when you stop waiting for it and make the most of the moment you are in now!"

– UNKNOWN

"To the mind that is still, the whole universe surrenders."

–LAO TZU

"The only journey
is the one within."

– RAINER MARIA RILKE

"Love the moment,
and the energy
of that moment
will spread beyond
all boundaries."

– CORITA KENT

COMMUNICATE FACE-TO-FACE

That friend you're about to email…don't. Pick up the phone or, even better, go and visit them in person instead.

TUNE INTO YOUR RHYTHM

Each of us has a natural rhythm. If you don't already know, work out whether you're an early bird, a night owl, or somewhere in between. When are you at your best? Instead of trying to fight your body's natural rhythms, embrace them and work them to your advantage.

"Learning how to be still, to really be still and let life happen - that stillness becomes a radiance."

– MORGAN FREEMAN

"Every day we should hear at least one little song, read one good poem, see one exquisite picture, and, if possible, speak a few sensible words."

– JOHANN WOLFGANG VON GOETHE

MAKE A MOOD JAR

This is a great meditation tool to use when you're stressed, and can also be used to calm children. All you need to do is place a mix of glue, glitter and warm water in a jam jar. Shake the jar. Imagine that the glitter is your thoughts scattered all over the place. Then watch the glitter settle and feel your thoughts doing the same.

"Peace of mind is not the absence of conflict from life, but the ability to cope with it."

– UNKNOWN

Smile!

"And now, this is the sweetest and most glorious day that ever my eyes did see."

– DONALD CARGILL

"There is no drug that can
do for you what eating well,
moving your body, self-love and
mindfulness can...fact!"

– BRIDGET JANE

"Today is the only day. Yesterday is gone."

– JOHN WOODEN

TAKE A MINDFUL SWIM

Swimming is a great way to combine exercise and mindfulness, as water has such therapeutic properties. As you swim, focus on your in- and out-breaths, and notice how the water supports your body. Notice the temperature of the water, the way it moves as your limbs glide gracefully through it. At the end of your swim, stay in the water for a few moments to rest. Close your eyes and listen to the water lapping around your limbs. Notice the way your muscles feel after the exercise.

"There is nothing
stronger in
the world than
gentleness."

– HAN SUYIN

Today, do something you've never done before.

MEDITATE ON DIFFICULT EMOTIONS

Find a quiet space to sit still and focus on your breathing. Let any negative thoughts and emotions you are experiencing wash over you, but instead of letting the thought or feeling overwhelm you, visualize it as a butterfly. Now watch the butterfly fluttering away from you.

"Enlightenment is always there. Small enlightenment will bring great enlightenment. If you breathe in and are aware that you are alive – that you can touch the miracle of being alive – then that is a kind of enlightenment."

– THÍCH NHẤT HẠNH

"Maybe you can afford to wait. Maybe for you there's a tomorrow. Maybe for you there's one thousand tomorrows, or three thousand, or ten, so much time you can bathe in it, roll around it, let it slide like coins through you fingers. So much time you can waste it. But for some of us there's only today. And the truth is, you never really know."

– LAUREN OLIVER

"I have come to accept the feeling of not knowing where I am going. And I have trained myself to love it. Because it is only when we are suspended in mid-air with no landing in sight, that we force our wings to unravel and alas begin our flight. And as we fly, we still may not know where we are going to. But the miracle is in the unfolding of the wings. You may not know where you're going, but you know that so long as you spread your wings, the winds will carry you."

– C. JOYBELL C.

BREATHE

A simple breathing exercise for calming the overworked mind is a timed breath where the exhale is longer than the inhale. Set a timer for 5 minutes. Inhale for a count of two, hold the breath in for a count of one. Exhale gently, counting out to four and finish by holding the breath out for a count of one. You can alter the breath lengths to suit you, the most important thing is that the exhale is longer than the inhale. Keep your breathing even and smooth.

"We can never obtain peace in the outer world until we make peace with ourselves."

– DALAI LAMA

TAKE A YOGA CLASS

Yoga encourages you to relax, slow your breath, and focus on the present, shifting the balance from the sympathetic nervous system (or the fight-or-flight response) to the parasympathetic nervous system. The latter is calming and restorative; it can lower your breathing and heart rate as well as decreasing blood pressure.

"Yoga practice can make us more and more sensitive to subtler and subtler sensations in the body. Paying attention to and staying with finer and finer sensations within the body is one of the surest ways to steady the wandering mind."

– RAVI RAVINDRA

"Pick the day. Enjoy it – to the hilt. The day as it comes. People as they come... The past, I think, has helped me appreciate the present, and I don't want to spoil any of it by fretting about the future."

– AUDREY HEPBURN

I WANT TO REMEMBER

Write an "I want to remember…" list. Choose little moments from today that you'd like to remember and note them down. This is a great way to ground you in what you love about your life.

MIND MAPPING

Mind mapping is a technique that creates visuals of your thoughts and helps unclutter your mind to bring focus and clarity. You can indulge in this cathartic process today by downloading a mind mapping app, or look for artistic inspiration online if you'd prefer to create your own visual masterpiece.

"Today is life – the only life you are sure of. Make the most of today."

– DALE CARNEGIE

"Not knowing how to feed the spirit, we try to muffle its demands in distraction...What matters is that one be for a time inwardly attentive."

— ANNE MORROW LINDBERGH

MINDFUL MOVEMENT MEDITATION

You don't have to remain still to meditate. Some people prefer to move, so try standing with your feet hip-width apart and allow your arms to hang down and relax. Bring awareness to your breathing. Then move your arms up in front of you as you breath in, and back down again as you breathe out. You can make up any sequence of movements that you'd like. As you do each sequence, focus on the bodily sensations resulting from the movements and keep your breathing even.

"Peace is something like happiness;
you cannot say, 'I will be happy when...'
and you can't say, 'I will be peaceful
when...' Your happiness shouldn't depend
on the situation you're in nor on the
circumstances that surround you. In
the same breath, you cannot wait for
everything around you to become peaceful
in order for you to say, 'I am peaceful.'
In both happiness and peace, there is
a heart of strength, determination and
steadfastness; a heart that has the power
to make things happen. You have to be at
peace. You have to be happy. Now."

– C. JOYBELL C.

EAT MINDFULLY

Today, when you eat your meals and snacks, eat mindfully. This approach involves bringing your full attention to the process of eating – to all the tastes, smells, thoughts and feelings that arise during a meal. Before you begin to eat, pause. Look at your food, inhale the scent. When you eat take small bites and chew slowly. Be fully present in the moment with your experience, savouring the tastes and textures one morsel at a time. By eating mindfully you can reclaim the pleasure of food.

"When walking,
walk.
When eating,
eat."

– ZEN PROVERB

"Never waste any amount of time doing anything important when there is a sunset outside that you should be sitting under!"

– C. JOYBELL C.

"In the midst of movement and chaos, keep stillness inside of you."

– DEEPAK CHOPRA

A MINDFUL SHOWER

Take a mindful shower this morning. Instead of the usual rush, notice the temperature of the water, and the feel of it in your hair, on your shoulders and running down your legs. Notice the smell of the soap and shampoo, and the sensation of them against your skin. Notice the water droplets on the shower screen, the water dripping down your body and the steam rising upwards. When thoughts arise, acknowledge them, let them be, and bring your attention back to the shower.

"Each morning when I open my eyes I say to myself: I, not events, have the power to make me happy or unhappy today. I can choose which it shall be. Yesterday is dead, tomorrow hasn't arrived yet. I have just one day, today, and I'm going to be happy in it."

– GROUCHO MARX

"Wisdom comes with the ability to be still. Just look and just listen. No more is needed."

– ECKHART TOLLE

PAUSE FOR BREATH

Throughout the day, pause for a moment and take ten slow, deep breaths. Focus on breathing out as slowly as possible, until the lungs are completely empty, and breathing in using your diaphragm. Notice the sensations of your lungs emptying and your ribcage falling as you breathe out. Notice what thoughts are passing through your mind. Observe those thoughts and feelings without judging them as good or bad, and without trying to change them, avoid them, or hold onto them. Simply observe them.

"Life isn't about waiting for the storm to pass...It's about learning to dance in the rain."

– VIVIAN GREENE

"Life isn't about getting and having, it's about giving and being."

– KEVIN KRUSE

"Today I will not be overwhelmed by panic. Panic will take my mind off my goals. It's normal to feel panic, but I simply feel it and let it go. I can get back on track by treading water until I regain my composure. I relax and know that all is well."

– MELODY BEATTIE

TUNE INTO BEAUTY

Take a moment to notice beauty around you. There's beauty in every home, street, office and in that person sitting opposite you at the table. Beauty comes in many forms, so pick something you find beautiful – tune fully into it and simply enjoy and appreciate the moment.

"Pause and remember – if you take the time to look for beauty, you will find it. Open yourself to the beauty you have been missing right before you."

– JENNI YOUNG

"Collect moments
not things."

– UNKNOWN

GROUNDING EXERCISE

Remove your shoes. Stand with your bare feet firmly on the ground, legs slightly apart, and allow your feet to really feel the support of the earth underneath you. Take a few moments to find a relaxed posture. Allow your in-breath and out-breath to fill your chest and abdominal area. Rest your gaze just ahead. Now focus your attention firstly on your feet, and then on the earth beneath your feet. Just feel the earth. Imagine that your feet have invisible roots pushing down into the earth. Push these roots as far as you can go.

MY MINDFUL MORNING

"Barefoot in the sparkling morning dew,
foraging, collecting and picking Mother Earth's gifts,
while cleansing my misty eyes.
The first burst of summer freshness
tingles on my still slumbering tongue,
whilst prickles shock my warm skin
into this reality with a 'here I am' cry.
A welcome breeze brushes my tousled hair,
back bent, knees muddy,
stretching and easing my morning stiffness.
Reaching for something
that gives me the energy for my day.
All this keeps me in touch,
with my place, in this space.
Being in the open arms of nature,
that nurture me and allow me to thrive.
This is how my day is born,
This is being alive."

– CHARLOTTE HILL

"Live simply.
Dream big.
Be grateful.
Give love.
Laugh lots."

– PAULO COELHO

"Don't wait for someone to bring you flowers. Plant your own garden and decorate your own soul."

– MÁRIO QUINTANA

REVIEW YOUR DAY

As your day concludes, spend a few mindful moments reviewing the day without judgment. Release whatever happened and file away the lessons learned. In this way, you will sleep more peacefully.

"One day, she realized that life was too short to worry about what might happen, so she decided to live in the moment and follow her heart."

– UNKNOWN

STOP

Try the STOP sign technique when responding to emails today:

S = Stop (do nothing)

T = Take a breath (or breathe until you're more relaxed)

O = Observe (What are you feeling and thinking?)

P = Proceed (when you feel calm again. Now you can respond if you need to)

"Whatever the present moment contains, accept it as if you had chosen it. Always work with it, not against it."

– ECKHART TOLLE

"Look deep into nature, and then you will understand everything better."

– ALBERT EINSTEIN

SLOW DOWN

You can do one task at a time, but also rush that task. Instead, take your time, and move slowly. Make your actions deliberate, not rushed and random. It takes practice, but it helps you focus on the task. You may think you don't have the time to slow down, but doing this can actually make you more productive.

"One of the greatest challenges in creating a joyful, peaceful and abundant life is taking responsibility for what you do and how you do it. As long as you can blame someone else, be angry with someone else, point the finger at someone else, you are not taking responsibility for your life."

– IYANLA VANZANT

"There are only two days in the year that nothing can be done. One is called yesterday and the other is called tomorrow, so today is the right day to love, believe, do and mostly live."

– DALAI LAMA

"Pause and remember – if you are reading this... You are blessed to be alive and today is a gift. Tomorrow is not guaranteed. Don't hesitate to forgive, hug and love those dear to you!"

– JENNI YOUNG

"Inner peace begins the moment you choose not to allow another person or event to control your emotions."

– UNKNOWN

GET COLOURING

Mandalas have been used in meditation for thousands of years. They are a simple geometric shape with no beginning or end. Within its circular shape, the mandala has the power to promote relaxation, balance the body's energies and enhance creativity and self-awareness. So today, reach for the felt-tip pens to colour in this beautiful mandala.

"Today is one of
your millions of
moments of bliss."

– KIMBERLEY BLAINE

"Look past your thoughts so you may drink the pure nectar of this moment."

– RUMI

"Make me strong in spirit, courageous in action, gentle of heart, let me act in wisdom, conquer my fear and doubt, discover my own hidden gifts, meet others with compassion, be a source of healing energies, and face each day with hope and joy."

– ABBY WILLOWROOT

"Hug somebody today you haven't hugged yet... It could change their day, their week, their life."

– MELINA ADDUCI

CLOUDS IN THE SKY MEDITATION

When you notice a thought come into your mind, just put the thought on a cloud as it drifts across the sky or dissipates. No judgments. The thoughts and feelings aren't good or bad. They just are.

"The most important decision you make is to be in a good mood."

– VOLTAIRE

"Life is too short to argue and fight with the past. Count your blessings, value your loved ones, and move on with your head held high."

– UNKNOWN

LET GO OF REGRETS

Today, make the positive life decision to let go of any regrets. Take 10 minutes out of your day to sit somewhere quiet and comfortable. Bring awareness to your breathing and reflect on any regrets you have, without letting them overwhelm you. See them as separate from your self. Now visualise these regrets floating away like balloons into the sky.

"We do not
remember days.
We remember
moments."

– CESARE PAVESE

"Those who are free of resentful thoughts surely find peace."

– BUDDHA

"Wherever you are, be there totally. If you find your here and now intolerable and it makes you unhappy, you have three options: remove yourself from the situation, change it, or accept it totally."

– ECKHART TOLLE

"You have power over your mind — not outside events. Realise this, and you will find strength."

– MARCUS AURELIUS

DO LESS

If you do less, you can do those things more slowly, more completely and with more concentration. If you fill your day with tasks, you will be rushing from one thing to the next without stopping to think about what you do. It's a matter of working out what's important, and letting go of what's not.

"No act of kindness, however small, is ever wasted."

– AESOP

"You can't calm the storm… so stop trying. What you can do is calm yourself. The storm will pass."

– TIMBER HAWKEYE

"Quit worrying about how
everything is going to turn out.
Live one day at a time; better yet,
make the most of this moment."

– JOEL OSTEEN

"When a new day begins, dare to smile gratefully!"

– STEVE MARABOLI

BE KIND TO YOURSELF

Today treat yourself to something you love – maybe indulge in your favourite food, read a good book in the bath, take a walk in a place you love, go dancing…Whatever you choose to do, be fully present in the wonderful moment in which you have rewarded yourself.

"Your mind is a flexible mirror, adjust it to see a better world."

– AMIT RAY

"Wherever you are,
be all there."

– JIM ELLIOT

"Miracles come in moments. Be ready and willing."

– WAYNE DYER

"When each day is the same as the next, it's because people fail to recognise the good things that happen in their lives every day."

– PAULO COELHO

USE YOUR OPPOSITE HAND

Today use your left hand if you're right-handed and vice versa. You will find yourself having to think about tasks you would normally perform mechanically and unthinkingly. Your brain will necessarily have to refocus on the present moment and the task in hand.

"Live one day at a time. Keep your attention in present time. Have no expectations. Make no judgements. And give up the need to know why things happen as they do. Give it up!"

– CAROLINE MYSS

RECOGNISE THE GOOD IN OTHERS

Today, project a positive spin on all your relationships and encounters. Look for the best in everyone you interact with. For every negative thought you associate with a person, think of something positive about them. In this way, you are inviting positivity into your own life.

"Leave footprints
of kindness
wherever you go."

– UNKNOWN

"Let today be the day you learn the grace of letting go and the power of moving on."

– STEVE MARABOLI

"You create a good future by creating a good present."

– ECKHART TOLLE

"There is a voice that doesn't use words — Listen!"

– RUMI

BRING AWARENESS TO YOUR POSTURE

Throughout the day bring your awareness to your posture. Whether you are sitting, lying down or standing, just bring all your attention to your body. This technique has an immediate grounding effect and restores our mindfulness. The aim is to simply be aware of the sensations that the body is feeling right at that moment. Try and remember to observe your posture and its sensations as often as you can throughout the day.

"Don't start your day with
the broken pieces of yesterday.
Every day is a fresh start.
Each day is a new beginning.
Every morning we wake up is
the first day of our new life."

– UNKNOWN

"The next message you need is always right where you are."

– RAM DASS

"The whole world opens when we accept this moment, this very moment."

– DEEPAK CHOPRA

CHECK YOUR HUNGER

Before reaching for your afternoon snack, check in by asking yourself whether you are stress eating or you're really hungry. This can help you to remain more mindful of your eating habits. Is your 3pm binge actually hunger, or is it really just a trigger to take a quick walk or timeout to de-stress?

"Writing letters is the purest
form of friendship we humans
can possibly possess. We capture
ourselves in a moment, and then we
give that moment to someone else."

– ANONYMOUS

"Taking time to do nothing often brings everything into perspective."

– DOE ZANTAMATA

"If you truly get in touch with a piece of carrot, you get in touch with the soil, the rain, the sunshine. You get in touch with Mother Earth and eating in such a way, you feel in touch with true life, your roots, and that is meditation. If we chew every morsel of our food in that way we become grateful and when you are grateful, you are happy."

– THÍCH NHẤT HẠNH

COOK MINDFULLY

Cooking provides a wonderful opportunity to be present, mindful and aware. As you prepare your food, notice the colours and textures. As your food cooks, listens to the sounds it makes – maybe oil sizzling, or water bubbling. Notice the smells that arise from each ingredient. Absorb these aromas. Try to recognise the smell of each ingredient in the dish. As your mind wanders, gently bring it back to your senses, to the sounds and smells of your cooking.

"Those who have one foot in the canoe, and one foot in the boat, are going to fall into the river."

– TUSCARORA

"You are free to think thoughts of worry or joy, and whatever you choose will attract the same kind back to you. Worry attracts worry. Joy attracts joy."

– RHONDA BYRNE

"Most of us experience a life full of wonderful moments and difficult moments. But for many of us, even when we are most joyful, there is fear behind our joy."

– THÍCH NHẤT HẠNH

"Let go of your thoughts, become still and alert, and don't try to understand or explain."

– ECKHART TOLLE

"Not all those who wander are lost."

– J.R.R. TOLKIEN

QUEUE MINDFULLY

This is about finding a moment of stillness amongst chaos. If you find yourself having to queue today, acknowledge the feelings of frustration or anger that may arise, but then bring awareness to your breathing; follow the course of the in-breath, all the way in and then the out-breath, all the way out. Take a moment to explore the sights around you and focus on something pleasant that you can see. Take a moment to savour this.

"Everything is falling together perfectly, even though it looks as if some things are falling apart. Trust in the process you are now experiencing."

– NEALE DONALD WALSCH

"It's very important that we re-learn the art of resting and relaxing. Not only does it help prevent the onset of many illnesses that develop through chronic tension and worrying; it allows us to clear our minds, focus, and find creative solutions to problems."

– THÍCH NHẤT HẠNH

"Without patience,
we will learn less in life.
We will see less.
We will feel less.
We will hear less.
Ironically,
rush and more
usually mean less."

– MOTHER TERESA

GO OUTSIDE

Being outdoors can relieve stress, while also improving energy levels, memory and attention. Even if you can only manage to get out for five minutes, it will give you a vital mental reboot.

"Somedays you just have to create your own sunshine."

– UNKNOWN

"The beauty you see in me is a reflection of you."

– RUMI

"There's a lot that is good in your life – don't take it for granted. Don't get so focused on the struggles that you miss the gift of today."

– JOEL OSTEEN

"Everything comes by being!
Be the love you seek.
Be the friend you seek.
Be the lover you seek.
Be the honesty you seek.
Be the integrity you seek.
Be the patience you seek.
Be the tolerance you seek.
Be the compassion you seek."

– BRYANT MCGILL

APPLY A FILTER TO YOUR LIFE

In other words, filter out all that is unnecessary. Sit quietly and bring awareness to your breathing. Visualise sand streaming through a sieve. The sand represents the flow of your life. Once all the sand has filtered through you are left with a pile of stones that won't fit through the small holes in the sieve. These stones represent the thoughts, feelings, people or objects that form some kind of obstacle in your life. Name these stones for what they are – one may be financial worries, another a friend who makes you feel bad… Then visualise throwing these stones into the sea and feel your unnecessary baggage sinking with them.

"If you don't make peace with your past, it will keep showing up in your present."

– WAYNE DYER

"Don't wait.
The time will never
be just right."

– NAPOLEON HILL

SELF-ESTEEM MANTRAS

Today bring the following mantras to mind whenever your confidence needs a boost:

'I am worth it,'

'I can do it,'

'I know who I am and I am enough.'

"The happiness of your life depends upon the quality of your thoughts."

– MARCUS AURELIUS

"Each day is an adventure in discovering the meaning of life."

– JACK CANFIELD

Today, practice a self-compassion exercise. The starting point is to bring to mind someone in your life who is precious to you. Imagine enfolding this person in loving-kindness, compassion and deep abiding care. Now see whether you can direct these feelings towards yourself with the following thoughts:

May I know a decrease in distress,

May I know some peace and tranquility in my life,

May I know some happiness and joy,

May I be confident that I can deal with my own suffering.

"To offer no resistance to life is to be in a state of grace, ease, and lightness."

– ECKHART TOLLE

"Perhaps ultimately, spiritual simply means experiencing wholeness and interconnectedness directly, a seeing that individuality and the totality are interwoven, that nothing is separate or extraneous. If you see in this way, then everything becomes spiritual in its deepest sense. Doing science is spiritual. So is washing the dishes."

– JON KABAT-ZINN

"People sacrifice the present for the future. But life is available only in the present. That is why we should walk in such a way that every step can bring us to the here and the now."

– THÍCH NHẤT HẠNH

"Since everything
is a reflection of our
minds… everything
can be changed by
our minds."

– BUDDHA

ONE-MINUTE EXERCISE

Sit in front of a clock or watch that you can use to time the passing of one minute. Your task is to focus your entire attention on your breathing, and nothing else, for the minute. Leave your eyes open and breathe normally. Be ready to catch your mind from wandering off (because it will) and return your attention to your breath whenever it does so.

"If we are peaceful, if we are happy, we can smile, and everyone in our family, our entire society, will benefit from our peace."

– THÍCH NHẤT HẠNH

"Surrender to what is. Let go of what was. Have faith in what will be."

– SONIA RICOTTI

"Be mindful of
your self-talk.
It's a conversation
with the universe."

– DAVID JAMES LEES

SLOW DOWN YOUR THOUGHTS

Find somewhere quiet and comfortable to sit. Bring awareness to your breathing and 'watch' the flitting thoughts as they race through your mind. Focus on your breathing. Check back in with your thoughts. Have they slowed a little? Keep going back to focus on your breathing until your thoughts have slowed or are still. This could take 5 minutes, 25 minutes or more. Be patient.

"The realisation that you have control and influence over your own life is a key concept you will need to understand to practice mindfulness."

– JANET LOUISE STEPHENSON

"The thing about
meditation is:
you become more
and more you."

– DAVID LYNCH

SPEND TIME ALONE

Try and spend some of today completely alone. Spending time on your own brings peace and nourishment to the soul. It can slow down your thoughts and make you feel more grounded in the present.

"You should sit in meditation
for twenty minutes every day –
unless you are too busy –
then you should sit for an hour."

– OLD ZEN ADAGE

"We have more possibilities available in each moment than we realise."

– THÍCH NHẤT HẠNH

CLEAR OUT YOUR WARDROBE

Today, cleanse your wardrobe. Recognise that by clearing out clothes you no longer need, you are letting go of the past. Getting rid of clothes you have kept because you may one day wear them again places you firmly in the present, rather than some distant unknown point in the future. Adopting a more minimalist approach to your wardrobe will simplify at least one area of your life.

"Restore your attention or bring it to a new level by dramatically slowing down whatever you're doing."

– SHARON SALZBERG

"You are the sky.
Everything else is
just the weather."

– PEMA CHÖDRÖN

"If you correct your mind, the rest of your life will fall into place."

– LAO TZU

SAY A SELECTIVE 'YES'

Today only say 'yes' to people and situations that support your wellbeing.

"Today me will live in the moment unless it's unpleasant, in which case me will eat a cookie."

– COOKIE MONSTER

"Just for today, allow yourself to embrace all that you are every moment. Know that you are a vessel of light. Allow yourself to release all doubts about your ability, the mistakes of the past, the fear of the future."

– IYANLA VANZANT

"Your experience of life isn't based on your life, but on what you pay attention to."

– GREGG KRECH

BANISH NEGATIVITY

Use a negative thought arising as a prompt to be mindful. When you recognise that you having such a thought, simple label it as negative. Visualise it as a piece of paper. Now scrunch it up and throw it in the bin. Now visualise being left with a completely blank piece of paper. Mentally write a positive thought on that page to replace the negative one you have just discarded.

"The most precious gift we can offer anyone is our attention. When mindfulness embraces those we love, they will bloom like flowers."

– THÍCH NHẤT HẠNH

DECREASE YOUR DISTRACTIONS

Today, pledge to decrease your distractions. Limit the time you spend watching television, don't respond to texts that aren't urgent, silence your phone for a while.

"Real generosity
toward the future
lies in giving all to
the present."

– ALBERT CAMUS

FIND YOUR HAPPY PLACE

To find your happy place think about who or what makes you incredibly happy. Your family? Friends? Travelling? A hobby you're passionate about? Walking beside the sea? Solitude or socialising? Take a moment to picture whatever or whoever makes you happy. Close your eyes, clear your mind and go to your happy place. What do you feel, hear, smell? Spend a few minutes there. Whenever the day gets tough, or you just need some timeout, tune in to your happy place again.

"Freedom is not given to us by anyone; we have to cultivate it ourselves. It is a daily practice...
No one can prevent you from being aware of each step you take or each breath in and breath out."

– THÍCH NHẤT HẠNH

"I got the blues thinking of the future, so I left off and made some marmalade. It's amazing how it cheers one up to shred oranges and scrub the floor."

– D.H. LAWRENCE

"Nothing is worth more than this day."

– JOHANN WOLFGANG VON GOETHE

"When we recognise the virtues, the talent, the beauty of Mother Earth, something is born in us, some kind of connection, love is born."

– THÍCH NHẤT HẠNH

LOOK OUT OF THE WINDOW

When we are busy indoors we seem to forget that we are part of the world outside. If you are working inside today, make the effort to look out of the window, even if only for a short while. This works particularly well if there is some nature outside to focus on – trees, flowers, birds or simply the clouds in the sky are all useful focal points to bring us back into the present moment.

"Realise deeply that the present moment is all you have. Make the NOW the primary focus of your life."

– ECKHART TOLLE

"We humans have lost the wisdom of genuinely resting and relaxing. We worry too much. We don't allow our bodies to heal, and we don't allow our minds and hearts to heal."

– THÍCH NHẤT HẠNH

"If you wait
for tomorrow,
tomorrow comes.
If you don't wait
for tomorrow,
tomorrow comes."

– SENEGALESE PROVERB

PREPARE FOR A GOOD NIGHT'S SLEEP

As you lie in bed tonight, bring awareness to your breathing for a few minutes. Then start to focus on a body part. As you focus on it clench the muscle and relax it, then move onto the next, working your way around the body. As your brain travels up your body, stop in each place to repeat the muscle clenching and relaxing. If your mind wanders, just gently bring it back to the body part.

"Rejoice in the things that are present; all else is beyond thee."

– MICHEL DE MONTAIGNE

"I am rooted,
but I flow."

– VIRGINIA WOOLF

"To meditate means to go home to yourself. Then you know how to take care of the things that are happening inside you, and you know how to take care of the things that happen around you."

– THÍCH NHẤT HẠNH

"Our goal should be to live life in radical amazement… get up in the morning and look at the world in a way that takes nothing for granted. Everything is phenomenal – everything is incredible – never treat life casually. To be spiritual is to be amazed."

– ABRAHAM JOSHUA HESCHEL

LEAVE NO TRACE

This is an exercise to increase awareness of the impact you have on your environment. The aim is to leave whatever room you have been in exactly the same, as if you had never been there. So, for example, if you are making dinner in the kitchen, clean up as you go along. If you have finished with your coffee cup, wash it up and put it away. Wipe up any spills you have made. Pick up anything you drop, and so on. By doing this, we are drawing away from our hurried nature, mindfully taking care of the little things that take care of us.

"I took a deep breath and listened to the old bray of my heart.
I am, I am, I am."

– SYLVIA PLATH

"I think it's very healthy to spend time alone. You need to know how to be alone and not be defined by another person."

– OSCAR WILDE

"Watch your thoughts;
they become words.
Watch your words;
they become actions."

– LAO TZU

"Let go of your mind and then be mindful. Close your ears and listen!"

– RUMI

LISTEN

We often confuse hearing for listening. Hearing is just perceiving the sounds around you. You can hear someone while typing a text message, for example. Listening is the intentional choice to fully pay attention to the other person – from the tone and texture of their voice to their emotional state and body language. Today, when you ask your loved one how their day was, for example, be sure to really listen. Take in what they're saying without projecting what you feel or expect onto their words.

"Today is a smooth white seashell, hold it close and listen to the beauty of the hours."

– ANON

"Mindfulness
isn't about getting
anywhere else."

– JON KABAT-ZINN

WRITE A LETTER

Today, write a letter to somebody you care about. Feel grounded and present as you write, and content in the knowledge that you are sharing this moment with someone who is important to you.

"There is nothing either good or bad but thinking makes it so."

– SHAKESPEARE

BE GRATEFUL

Create a mental list of things in your life for which you are grateful – even better, write them down.

"This very moment is the perfect teacher, and, lucky for us, it's with us wherever we are."

– PEMA CHÖDRÖN

"It is nothing to die. It is frightful not to live."

– VICTOR HUGO

"We will be more successful in all our endeavours if we can let go of the habit of running all the time, and take little pauses to relax and re-centre ourselves. And we'll also have a lot more joy in living."

– THÍCH NHẤT HẠNH

"You must learn a new way to think before you can master a new way to be."

– MARIANNE WILLIAMSON

MINDFUL WASHING UP

Any mundane household task can be transformed into a mindful meditation. Simply by grounding yourself in the moment and completing each task slowly and intentionally, you can bring a sense of calm to the proceedings. Wash one item at a time and focus on what you're doing. What does the water feel like on your hands? The smell of the washing up liquid, the play of the light on the water, the feel of the cloth against the plate…If your mind wanders, simply bring it back to the task in hand.

"We shape clay into a pot, but it is the emptiness inside that holds what we want."

– UNKNOWN

"All negativity is caused by an accumulation of psychological time and denial of the present. Unease, anxiety, tension, stress, worry — all forms of fear — are caused by too much future, and not enough presence. Guilt, regret, resentment, grievances, sadness, bitterness, and all forms of non-forgiveness are caused by too much past, and not enough presence."

– ECKHART TOLLE

"Because of your smile, you make life more beautiful."

– THÍCH NHẤT HẠNH

TAKE A WALK

Solvitur ambulando is Latin for "it is solved by walking." Today, go for a walk, preferably somewhere away from the crowds. It is an excellent way to calm the mind, gain new perspective and facilitate greater awareness.

"A mind is like a parachute. It doesn't work if it isn't open."

– FRANK ZAPPA

"You practice mindfulness, on the one hand, to be calm and peaceful. On the other hand, as you practice mindfulness and live a life of peace, you inspire hope for a future of peace."

– THÍCH NHẤT HẠNH

"You can make any human activity into meditation simply by being completely with it and doing it just to do it."

– ALAN W. WATTS

FOCUS ON NATURE

Pick a natural organism within your immediate environment and focus on watching it for a minute or two. This could be a leaf or an insect, the clouds or the moon. Don't do anything except notice the thing you are looking at. But really notice it. Look at it as if you are seeing it for the first time. Visually explore every aspect of this glorious element of the natural world. Allow your spirit to connect with its role and purpose in the world. Allow yourself just to notice and "be".

"Nothing ever gets anywhere.
The earth keeps turning round and
gets nowhere. The moment is the
only thing that counts."

– JEAN COCTEAU

"We do not heal the past by dwelling there. We heal the past by living in the present."

– MARIANNE WILLIAMSON

END THE DAY ON A POSITIVE NOTE

Write down three positive things that have happened to you today. This will help you recognise that good things have happened, however small, and will keep you grounded in the best aspects of your life.

"We need enlightenment, not just individually but collectively, to save the planet. We need to awaken ourselves. We need to practice mindfulness if we want to have a future, if we want to save ourselves and the planet."

– THÍCH NHẤT HẠNH

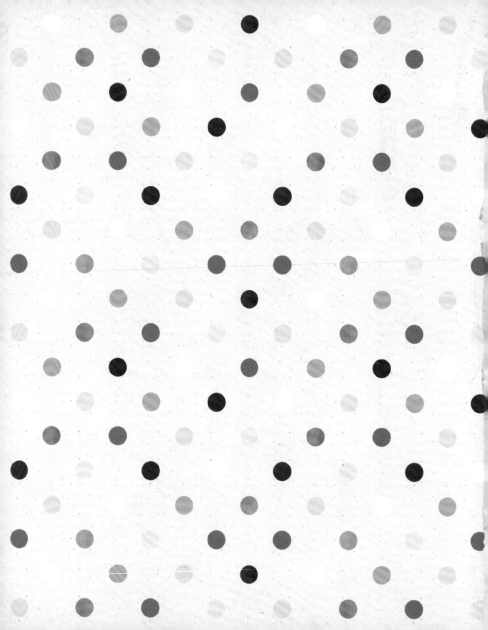